Life's *Reflections:*
A Collections of Poems

Serenity, Peace and Faith

DR. VERNITA BLACK

ISBN: Softcover   978-1-5245-7958-6
         EBook   978-1-5245-7959-3

Print information available on the last page

Rev. date: 02/03/2017

To order additional copies of this book, contact:
Xlibris
1-888-795-4274
www.Xlibris.com
Orders@Xlibris.com

Table of Contents

This collection of poems has been inspired by Dr. Vernita Black's life's reflections of poetry. They have been written from the heart and are filled with love, peace and joy. During the last decades of my life, I have written a collection of poetry and would like to share some of them with you. Poetry has given me thepower of hope, strength, gratitude and inspiration and helped me find meaning in our busy world through reflection. Poetry has given me an opportunity to take a deep breath and feel the beauty of the world. No matter what might be going on around us, it is still possible to see beauty.

Dreams

I travel to a place where I'm all alone

No one can bother me while I'm on my own

No noise, threats, anger or danger

No worries or concerns about meeting strangers

It's full of beauty, peace, serenity and joy

It's a place where I can go and no one can destroy

I'm safe and protected from chaos, turmoil and fears

No stress, concerns and not a drop of tears

I don't want to wake from this glorious place

It's simply beautiful and full of grace

Now it's time to do my best

This is a place where I can get plenty of rest

Life is beautiful and this I know

Dreams are someplace that will help me grow

Hope

Hope is the light that shines at the end of the road

It brings great pleasure and lifts the load

The race is complete when you've crossed the line

You are finally relaxed and everything is fine

Keep the hope today and always as you continue to climb

And you will see, you are right on time

Don't be concern about the past

Hope is something that will truly last

Faith

As I travel through the day, I firmly believe

that faith will guide me along the way

Without any worries or struggles that can send me astray

When the pain comes, I hold on to faith

knowing that it will not go away

My faith is truly here to stay

Peace

Feel the presence of peace surrounding me from head to toe

It's beautiful and lovely and I enjoy it so

My body is like feathers filled with peace

All I want is for it to increase

Relax if you must I will not say a word

Peace is something that I like and it is for sure preferred

Change

When you are weary and don't know what to do

Change your thoughts this will get you through

Without change it is hard to grow

If you don't change you will never know

Let go of the past and look ahead

You will feel the change of your future instead

As you can see that change is for the best

Now is the time for you to get plenty of rest

I Believe

My pain troubles me day-to-day, still I believe

My heart is heavy, still I believe

My feet hurts, still I believe

I can't hardly walk, still I believe

My breath is shallow, still I believe

My tears are flowing, still I believe

My life is dark, still I believe

My life is peaceful, still I believe

My life is glorious, still I believe

My life is full of God's presence, still I believe

Anger

I am angry because that's what I choose to do

No one can make me angry not even you

The anger hurts that I have in my heart

Even when you leave me and we are apart

The anger is internal and only I can control

Not even you can't console

I must work with my anger each and everyday

All I need to do is continue to pray

My anger gets better as the days go by

All I can do is to look toward the sky

Pain

The pain is real for it comes and goes

Don't under estimate it, this I know

I walk around with it all the time

I feel as though I've committed a crime

The pain is real for me too

I'm human and lovable just like you

All I ask of you is to see me through

As I wonder about on the floor

Please don't shut me out and close the door

I walk with pain morning noon and night

With no help and not a person in sight

I close my eyes and pray to God for help every day

I've been blessed with his presence as he helps me to pray

I have nothing else in this life to gain

For this helps me to ease the pain

Hatred

Don't hate me because of the color of my skin

Everyone has the chance in this life to win

Don't hate me for knowing the way

I will help

you if you are willing to pray

Don't hate me because I've tried

You have no idea how much I've cried

Don't hate me for moving ahead

Don't hate me because you choose to do something else instead

Don't' hate me for what I have done thus far

Don't hate me because you too can be a star

Don't hate me because I have the ability to see

Don't hate me because I am only trying to be me

It's A Miracle

It's a miracle when you can suddenly walk

It's a miracle when you start to talk

It's a miracle when you hear the birds sing

It's a miracle when the church bells ring

It's a miracle when the pain goes away

It's a miracle when the doctor says you no longer have to stay

It's a miracle when you escape death

It's a miracle when you take that breath

It's a miracle when you start to see

It's a miracle when you have learned that life is beautiful as can be

It's a miracle when everything is alright

It's a miracle when God is present in your sight

Listen my Child

Good morning my child

Today is your day to see the light

Without much effort to put up a fight

You see my child it's your turn to be brave

There is no need to ever be a slave

When you feel an urge to reach out

Don't hesitate to use your clout

There is always that star within the sky

Looking for you to aim high

Hold your head up and continue to see the light

You see my child there's always that star within your sight

As The Days Go By

As the days, evenings and nights go by from day to day

We must all continue to stick together as clay

It does not matter what race you are nor the color of your skin

You must strive each and every day in life to win

Set your limits to the sky

Remember to always aim very high

Ask a friend to help you out

They too may have some clout

It does not matter if you are male, female, black or white

Just work together and do it right

We must work together every day

This is how love can be here to stay

Life

Enjoy life as much as you can

It has a beginning, middle and end

Cherish each and every moment as you wake

It's wonderful and beautiful for goodness sake

Don't take it for granted, it moves so fast

Embrace the peace and enjoy it while it last

Take a deep breath and feel the presence of the serenity

and calmness around you

It's your time and you are due

Relax and let go of the hurt and pain for you have plenty to gain

There's glorious things ahead, it's time to release the chain

Surrender to him and ask for peace

He will deliver and never cease

Continue to walk in that path of hope

You will see how beautiful and lovely it will be to cope

Grateful

I'm grateful for you Lord today

At peace and comfort and here to stay

My heart is filled with joy, peace and love

Thanking you for your presence for the man above

I will continue to walk in your path each and everyday

All I ask is for your help as I continue to pray

I am grateful for you in showing me the way

For I am here dear Lord to serve you everyday

Stand Firm

I stand firm no matter what comes my way

You can't hurt me because I am here to stay

I am strong tenacious and intelligent in everything I do

If you stand in my way, I will help you too

Walk with your head up no matter how you feel

Just believe and you will be healed

I stand firm as I continue to fight

It won't be long before I see the light

Move forward as I continue to stand

Before long I will reach that land

The stars are shining big and bright

Oh my goodness what a beautiful sight

I stand firm with no regrets

I am willing, able and ready to reset

I am standing firm each and everyday

Move over and don't get in my way

Soldier Of God

I am a soldier of God for peace, serenity and love

I am a soldier of God for the beauty and the presence of God above

I am opened and receptive to what comes my way

I am a soldier of God who loves to pray

I am a soldier of God that's willing to lend

I am a soldier of God that will be your friend

I am a soldier of God who knows what it is all about

I am a soldier of God that will be there without a shallow of a doubt

Angels

Angels are watching over us all the time

No worries that they won't be there in the drop of a dime

Get in tune with your mind, heart and soul

You will be filled with peace and completely whole

Angels are wondering above and won't make a sound

They are peaceful, serene and all around

Feel the presence as they go to and from

Don't hesitate when you see them come

Enjoy the moment and make it last

It is something that you don't want to past

It's alright if the stay is brief in your sight

Angels presence is letting you know that everything will be alright

Live your life to the fullest each and everyday

Angels are there as you continue to pray.

Blessed

Blessed to be alive

Blessed to continue to strive

Blessed to breath air

Blessed to be able to sit in a chair

Blessed to wake up today

Blessed and grateful to continue to pray

Blessed to be able to write

Blessed to be able to hold on tight

Military Travels

Here we are dear Lord on our way

As you help this crew and our family to pray

I know everything will be just fine

I know you will keep everything in line

When things start to seem not just so right

Hold on and hold on tight

Because you taught us and taught us oh so well

We will try not to worry because we know you can tell

I know you will be there through thick and thin

Oh yes, Oh yes at the drop of a pin

So let's go for a ride

As God takes us through the tides

Now let's keep our faith and continue to be strong

Before long God will take us back where we belong

Hawaii

Thank you God for giving me this opportunity today

Although I know many would want to stay

It's ok that we really had to cut our time

Because we know you will keep us on your mind

Surely, there will be better plans ahead

I choose to follow you instead

Hawaii was a lovely place to see

I thank you dear Lord for this one day which was simply lovely as can be

I'm ready for whatever you have in store

I know in my heart I will truly adore

Guam

I have faith in God with all my might

I keep him in my presence in a clear and glorious sight

He always seems to make a way

As he did for us today

Although Guam was a short stay

God managed for us to spend the day

Surely, there was a reason for our delay

God made a way for all of us today

So let's thank him for giving us this chance

Even though, it was only for a glance

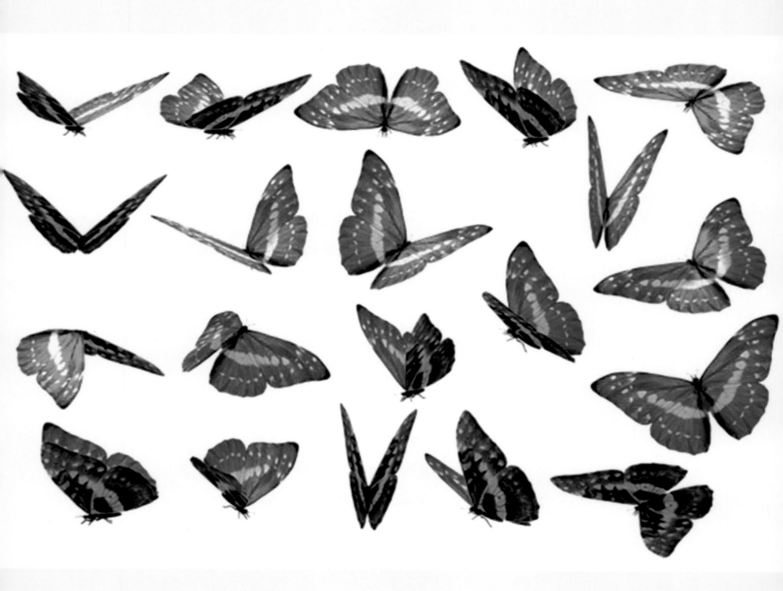

Butterflies

I fly with passion and grateful wings

With peace and beauty that life always brings

I spread my wings as I wonder through the sky

Life is beautiful as I come around

I promise you I will not make a sound

Pay attention to my presence as I come about from near and far

I will protect you wherever you are

I Can And So Can You

Yes, you're wondering why I'm proud to be an American woman of today.

Well, I'll tell you because there's plenty to say

I represent the women in today's society, because I can, I can and I can

Yes, I can do and accomplish many things because I am willing
and able to stretch above negativity, hatred, and weakness

My feelings are strong, powerful and naturally there's kindness

I have and you have the power, the vision and grace
to do all things that strengthens us

You too, as an American woman of today can help anoint
that same principle, power and glory in this nation

The doors are opened for you in this very land

We must all take the first step in helping someone who seems
to be sinking deep, deep, deep within that sand

Yes, I say again, I am, I am a proud American woman of today

So, come walk with me, talk with me and work with me

The power is given to each and every one who has the vision to see

We may say without struggle there is no progress, but we
must first except it, acknowledge it and believe it

The power is given to each and every one of us, whether black or white

But now is the time to vision the thoughts and things
that makes a difference within our sight

Until then, I'll see you on the other side of the hill

So let's go forth and peace be still

Try God

Sometimes things may seem so unfair

Then you wonder if anyone really cares

So, you say, maybe or maybe not

But the answer is God is all we really got

So, when you feel that urge to frown

Try him, he won't let you down

So now's the time to get on our knee

Oh yes, we must pray indeed

Just remember God is by our side each and everyday

All he asks is for us to continue to pray

It was a late afternoon when they laid him in the tomb

He suffered, died and rose again on the third day

That's so wonderful to know that my God is here and here to stay

To him I pray

Jesus Lives

Jesus died to help us all

With such pain whether big or small

Have you ever wondered what it's all about?

I do without a shadow of a doubt

The nails were driven in his feet and hands

Like they had no pity and they had rehearsed the plan

Yet, many could not understand what Jesus was about

They cried, wept, and some even shouted out

My Lord, My Lord, why aren't you able to help yourself today

He spoke softly, forgive them for they know not what they do,

and the people watched as Jesus passed away

Still Standing

You may say that it's over for me, but I am still standing

and happy as can be

You may think that I don't have the ability to see

I am still standing and feeling very free

You may say that I am not beautiful or smart

I am still standing with love in my heart

You may say that I am old and beat up

I am still standing no matter what

You may say that I don't have a clue

I am still standing what can you do

You may say that my pain won't go away

I am still standing what can I say

Thank You God

Thanks God for giving me the strength

Through the good and bad times no matter what length

I greatly appreciate your patience with me

Even the times when I could not see

I will continue to do my best to be strong

Regardless of what people say and when things go wrong

Even when times may appear to be really rough

I will remember that I must continue to be tough

So thank you for making me aware

This helps me dear Lord to grow and to share

Poetry has always enriched and inspired our lives, especially in uncertain situations of chaos, turmoil and the stress of today's world.

Nevertheless, hope can always be found in whatever situation we face.

I hope these poems have touched your heart in some way, perhaps opening your eyes to have faith, peace or just the pure love for family, friends or country. Whatever it is, use it for yourself or share it with someone else. May you have continued blessings and peace now and always.

Hope

"Continue to move forward no matter what comes your way, take one step at a time"

Dr. Vernita Black

Printed in the United States
By Bookmasters